Copy 1

J
746.443
GRE   Greenoff, Jane
               Cross stitch farmyard / Jane Greenoff. --
           Devon : David & Charles, 1994.
               32 p : col. ill. ; 27 cm. -- (Crafts for kids)

               Includes index.
               c1 So. Eastern 11-2-95 $9.95.
               ISBN 0-7153-0248-5.

318

           1.Cross-stitch - Patterns.   I.Title.

1195 sja

CROSS STITCH FARMYARD

Jane Greenoff

David & Charles

To my children, James Eric and Louise Estelle with love always

A DAVID & CHARLES BOOK

Copyright text, designs and charts © Jane Greenoff 1994
Copyright photographs © David & Charles 1994

First published 1994

A catalogue record for this book is available from the British Library.

ISBN 0 7153 0248 5

Typeset by ABM Typographics Ltd Hull
and printed in Italy
by LEGO SpA
for David & Charles
Brunel House Newton Abbot Devon

contents

how to stitch

Counted cross stitch is one of the easiest types of embroidery.

All the charted designs are made up of squares which you reproduce on your fabric as cross stitches. In the next section [page 6] you will see how to read a chart.

YOU WILL NEED

To work a design from this book you will need threads, Aida fabric 11 blocks to 2.5cm [1 inch] and a blunt tapestry needle, size 24 or 22.

Some stitchers like to use a hoop or frame when they are working cross stitch. It is not essential for this type of work.

All the designs in the book were worked without a frame.

THE THREADS

All the stitched designs in this book have been worked in stranded cottons (floss). Each length of thread is made up of six strands of cotton (floss) and you usually divide the strands before you start sewing.

All the cross stitch in this book is stitched using three strands of stranded cotton (floss).

It is a good idea to 'organise' your threads. Cut the threads into manageable lengths [50cm or 20 inches] and loop them on to a piece of punched card. This helps to stop tangles and knots.

THE FABRIC

All the designs in this book are stitched on 11 count Aida fabric. It is made of cotton and is specially woven for cross stitch. It looks as if it is made up of squares, which makes the counting much easier.

All the designs in the book are stitched from the centre of the fabric, which means you actually get the design in the middle. This is very important when you are ready to frame the finished piece.

The fabric used for cross stitch does tend to fray around the edges, so it is a good idea to neaten the edge in some way. Either fold over and stitch a narrow hem or oversew the edge loosely. This stitching can be pulled out when the work is finished.

HOW TO STITCH

Find the centre of the fabric, which is where you begin stitching. To do this, fold the fabric in half, then in half again and press lightly. Work a line of tacking (basting) stitches along the folds, as shown opposite. The lines meet at the centre, marking the position of the first stitch. (Remove the tacking carefully after the cross stitch design is finished.)

Divide the strands of cotton (floss) and thread your needle with three strands.

Look at picture A opposite. Bring the needle up at point 1 (but at the centre of the fabric).

Leave a short end on the wrong side [see picture B].

Cross the square and go down through point 2.

Come up again at point 3.

Cross the square and go down through point 4. Note the position of the needle. Repeat, to make a row of half crosses.

Complete the cross stitches as shown in C. As you work each cross stitch on the material, it matches one square on the chart.

To prevent the loose ends from undoing themselves, you will need to finish them off as you go. It is better not to use knots as they cause lumps and bumps that show on the front when the work is finished.

After working a few stitches, turn the work over to the wrong side and catch in the thread left at the start [see picture D].

When you have finished one colour, finish off the ends in the same way [see picture E].

Picture F shows that the top stitch should face the same way whether you are working up and down or from left to right.

Picture G illustrates how to add the backstitch outline around blocks of colour.

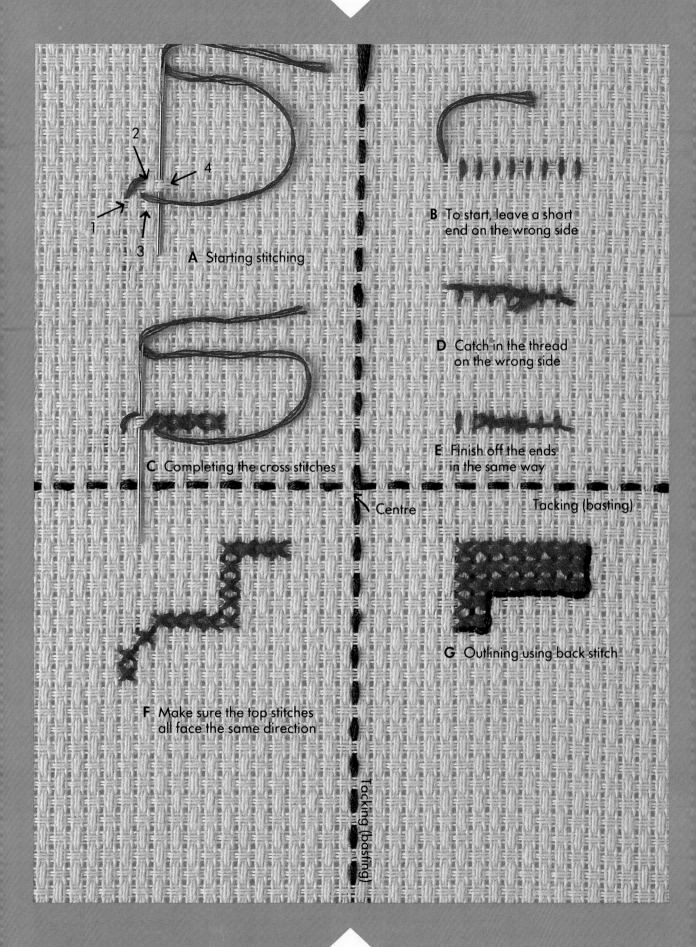

A Starting stitching

B To start, leave a short end on the wrong side

C Completing the cross stitches

D Catch in the thread on the wrong side

E Finish off the ends in the same way

Centre

Tacking (basting)

F Make sure the top stitches all face the same direction

G Outlining using back stitch

Tacking (basting)

how to read a chart

On the page opposite you will see a large coloured chart of the pink pig.
This design is illustrated in the colour photograph on page 9. Full stitching instructions are on page 8.
The pink pig chart is drawn in felt-tip pens on squared paper.
Each square on the paper represents one square on your fabric. As we discovered in the picture on page 5, the Aida fabric used for all the stitching in this series of books is also made up of squares.
All the charts in the book are drawn in the same way. Each one has a key showing a list of thread colours used next to the symbols used on the chart. The pink pig design uses pink, pale peach, green, brown, grey and a grey outline.
The central stitch is marked on the chart. You can see that the first stitch on the pink pig is pink. As with each project, the stitching instructions for the pink pig tell you where to start and in which direction to stitch. You will soon get the idea.
All the symbols are worked in cross stitch in the colours listed in the key. You can use any colour or brand of thread you like, but if you want to copy the design in the colour photograph exactly, you will need to use DMC stranded cotton (floss). The DMC shade numbers are included in each project, along with Anchor numbers for people who prefer to use Anchor threads.
The solid outlines around the stitching are worked in back stitch when the cross stitch has been completed [see pages 4 and 5]. You can see that the outline of the pink pig is stitched in grey.

notes for parents and teachers

Counted cross stitch is one of the simplest, least expensive and most rewarding types of needlecraft and is suitable for children of all ages and both sexes!

My own experience of teaching children under ten has been a revelation. The children concerned were all volunteers after school hours and were mostly boys. After learning the basic stitch, all the children were keen to stitch and design for themselves.

The most successful children were those whose first projects were small and quickly completed. They were therefore eager to experiment.

HOW TO HELP
1 Choose small projects with large blocks of colour.
2 Select fabric that can be seen clearly and handled easily.
   Aida fabric is available in 8, 11, 14, 16 and 18 blocks to 2.5cm [1 inch]. All projects in this book use 11 count Aida.
3 Use blunt tapestry needles with large eyes in size 24 or 22.
4 Be prepared to thread and re-thread needles to start with. You may find it helpful to have a number of threaded needles ready for use.

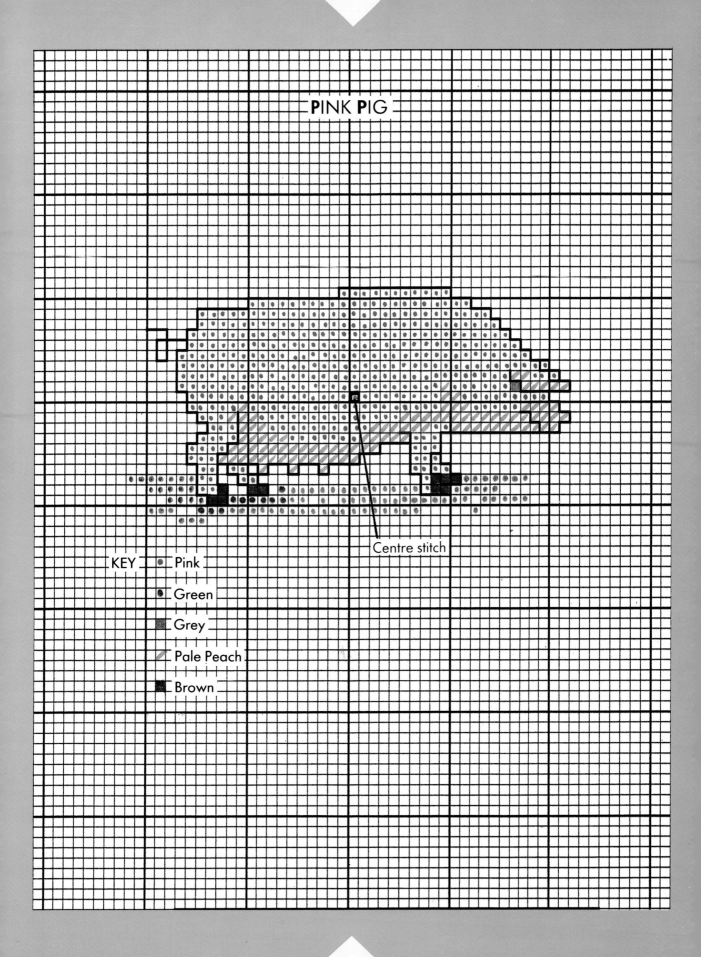

PINK PIG

Centre stitch

KEY
- ● Pink
- ● Green
- ▨ Grey
- ╱ Pale Peach
- ■ Brown

PINK PIG

THREADS

COLOUR	DMC	ANCHOR
Pink	352	09
Green	367	0216
Grey	317	0400
Pale peach	353	06
Brown	407	0914

STITCHING INSTRUCTIONS

● Cut a piece of Aida fabric not less than 25 x 20cm [10 x 8 inches] and hem the raw edges to prevent fraying [see page 4].

● Remember that all the projects in this book were stitched on 11 count Aida. This means that there are 11 stitches to 2.5cm [1 inch].

● Mark the centre of the fabric with lines of tacking stitches [see page 5].

● Thread your needle with three strands of pink stranded cotton (floss) and look at the chart on page 7. Work the marked central stitch in pink and, working towards the pig's snout, keep the top stitch of each cross stitch facing in the same direction [see page 5]. To make the work easier, you can turn it upside down and work towards the pig's back, but remember to turn the chart the same way.

● Work all the pink. Then, using the pale peach, add the pig's tummy and ears.

● Continue working all the cross stitches in the same way, finishing off the ends as you go [see page 5].

● When the cross stitch is complete, remove the tacking threads marking the centre, check for missed stitches and then add the outlining.

OUTLINING

● Thread your needle with two strands of grey stranded cotton (floss). Add the outline in back stitch, following the chart and working around the pig as shown in the photograph.

● Using two strands of grey, add the pig's curly tail in back stitch.

Note: The pink pig is part of the farmyard scene at the front of the book and the pig family on page 27 [see Design for Yourself, page 24].

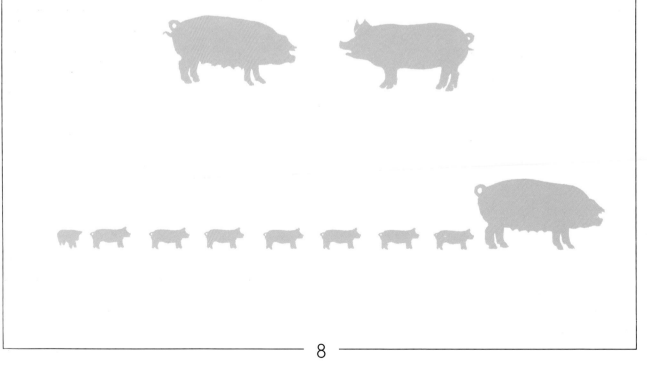

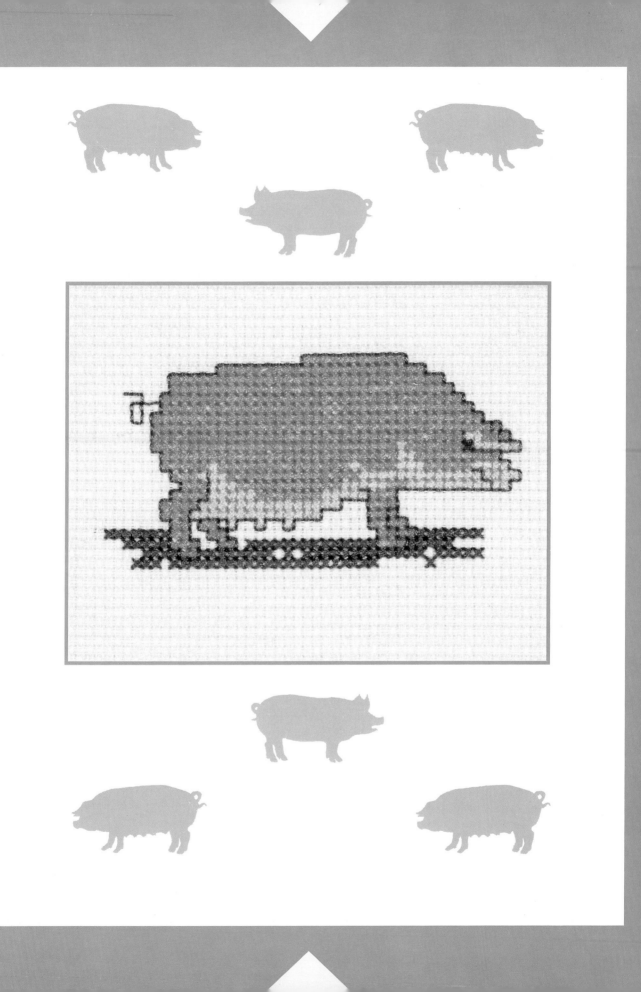

DUCK FAMILY

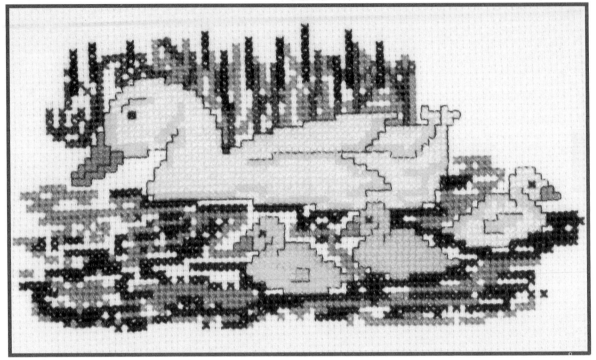

THREADS

COLOUR	DMC	ANCHOR
Brown	898	0381
Cream	712	0926
Light blue	932	0343
Dark blue	930	0922
Dark yellow	743	0305
Pale yellow	727	0293
Orange	722	0323
Dark green	562	0210
Mid green	368	0214

STITCHING INSTRUCTIONS

● Cut a piece of Aida fabric not less than 30 x 20cm [12 x 8 inches] and hem the raw edges to prevent fraying [see page 4].

● Mark the centre of the fabric with lines of tacking stitches [see page 5].

● Thread your needle with three strands of cream stranded cotton (floss), look at the chart and, starting from the marked central stitch, work across towards the duck's neck and head, keeping the top stitch of each cross stitch facing in the same direction.

● Add the dark yellow around the duck's face, then add the orange for her beak.

● Complete the mother duck, then add her ducklings.

● Stitch the water in your own pattern using dark and light blue. Add the reeds and bull rushes if liked.

● Continue working all the cross stitches in the same way, finishing off the ends as you go [see page 5].

● When the cross stitch is complete, remove the tacking threads marking the centre, check for missed stitches and then add the outlining.

OUTLINING

● Thread your needle with two strands of brown stranded cotton (floss) and add the outline in back stitch [see page 5].

DUCK FAMILY

KEY

Brown
Cream
Light blue
Dark blue
Dark yellow
Pale yellow
Orange
Dark green
Mid green

RED TRACTOR

THREADS

COLOUR	DMC	ANCHOR
Dark grey	413	0401
Black	310	0403
Dark red	814	045
Yellow	725	0306
Bright red	321	046
Green	562	0216

STITCHING INSTRUCTIONS

● Cut a piece of Aida fabric not less than 30 x 24cm [12 x 10 inches] and hem the raw edges to prevent fraying [see page 4].

● Mark the centre of the fabric with lines of tacking stitches [see page 5].

● Thread your needle with three strands of dark red stranded cotton (floss), look at the chart and, starting from the marked central stitch, work towards the front of the tractor, keeping the top stitch of each cross stitch facing in the same direction.

● Using the bright red, work the bonnet towards the cab.

● Continue working all the cross stitches, in the same way, finishing off the ends as you go [see page 5] and, leaving the stitches worked in black to the end. This prevents the fabric being marked should you have to unpick any mistakes! Black stranded cotton (floss) sometimes leaves a shadow.

● When the cross stitch is complete, remove the tacking threads marking the centre, check for missed stitches and then add the outlining.

OUTLINING

● Thread your needle with two strands of black stranded cotton (floss) and add the outline in back stitch [see page 5].

● Using two strands of black, add the steering wheel, the fuel cap on the bonnet and the top of the engine.

● Note: The red tractor is also worked as part of the farmyard scene at the front of the book [see Design for Yourself, page 24].

RED TRACTOR

Centre stitch

BLACK AND WHITE COW

THREADS

COLOUR	DMC	ANCHOR
Pink	754	0881
Black	310	0403
Dark stone	640	0393
Dark grey	413	0401
Cream	712	0926
Dark green	367	0216
Light green	320	0215

STITCHING INSTRUCTIONS

● Cut a piece of pink Aida fabric not less than 25 x 14cm [10 x 6 inches] and hem the raw edges to prevent fraying [see page 4].

● Mark the centre of the fabric with lines of tacking stitches [see page 5].

● Thread your needle with three strands of black stranded cotton (floss), look at the chart and, starting from the marked central stitch, work towards the cow's head.

● You can choose which colour you work next, remembering to keep the top stitch of each cross stitch facing in the same direction.

● Continue working all the cross stitches in the same way, finishing off the ends as you go [see page 5].

● When the cross stitch is complete, remove the tacking threads marking the centre, check for missed stitches and then add the outlining.

OUTLINING

● Thread your needle with two strands of black stranded cotton (floss), add the outline in back stitch around the cow's body, then add her tail.

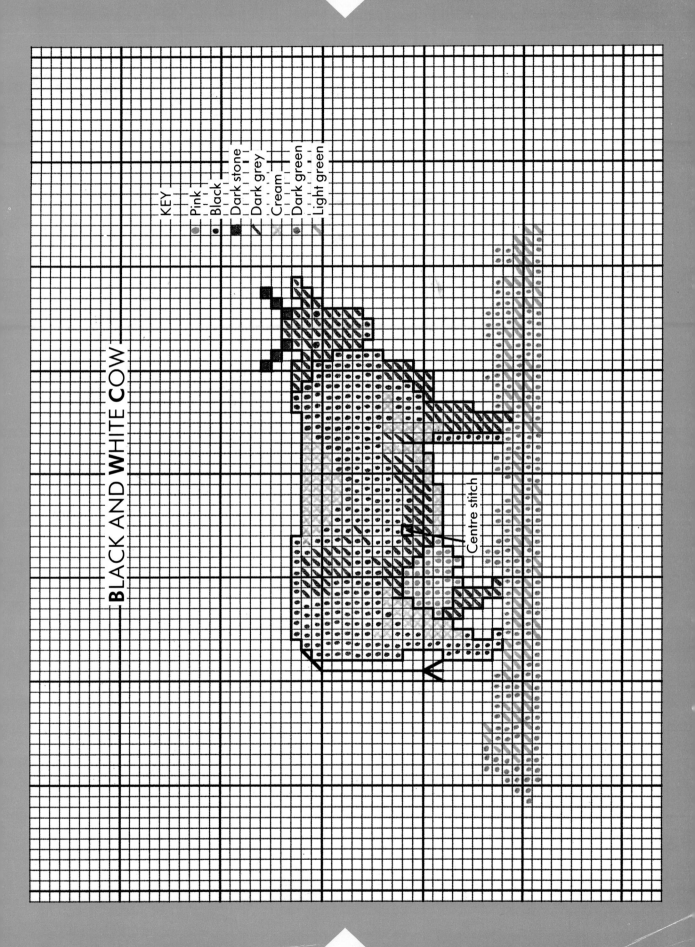

BLACK AND WHITE COW

KEY
Pink
Black
Dark stone
Dark grey
Cream
Dark green
Light green

Centre stitch

BILLY GOAT

THREADS

COLOUR	DMC	ANCHOR
Dark green	367	0216
Light green	368	0214
Chestnut	407	0914
Dark blue	930	0922
Coffee	437	0375
Honey	738	0372
Dark brown	898	0381

The billy goat has quite a lot of shading in his shaggy coat, but you can stitch him quite simply by mixing colours. This is very easy to do. When you thread your needle you use more than one shade of thread, and this gives a nice speckled appearance to the stitching without having to change colours after just a few stitches.

STITCHING INSTRUCTIONS

Cut a piece of Aida fabric not less than 25 x 25cm [10 x 10 inches] and hem the raw edges to prevent fraying [see page 4].

Mark the centre of the fabric with lines of tacking stitches [see page 5].

Thread your needle with two strands of coffee and one of honey stranded cotton (floss) together, look at the chart and, starting from the marked central stitch, work across and down towards the goat's legs, keeping the top stitch of each cross stitch facing in the same direction.

When you have finished this needleful, try another combination of colours. You will see the billy goat's coat looks more natural than if worked in just one colour.

Continue working all the cross stitches finishing off the ends as you go [see page 5].

When the cross stitch is complete, remove the tacking threads marking the centre, check for missed stitches and then add the outlining.

OUTLINING

Thread your needle with two strands of dark brown stranded cotton (floss) and add the outline in back stitch around the billy goat.

Using two strands of dark brown add the outline to the horns in back stitch.

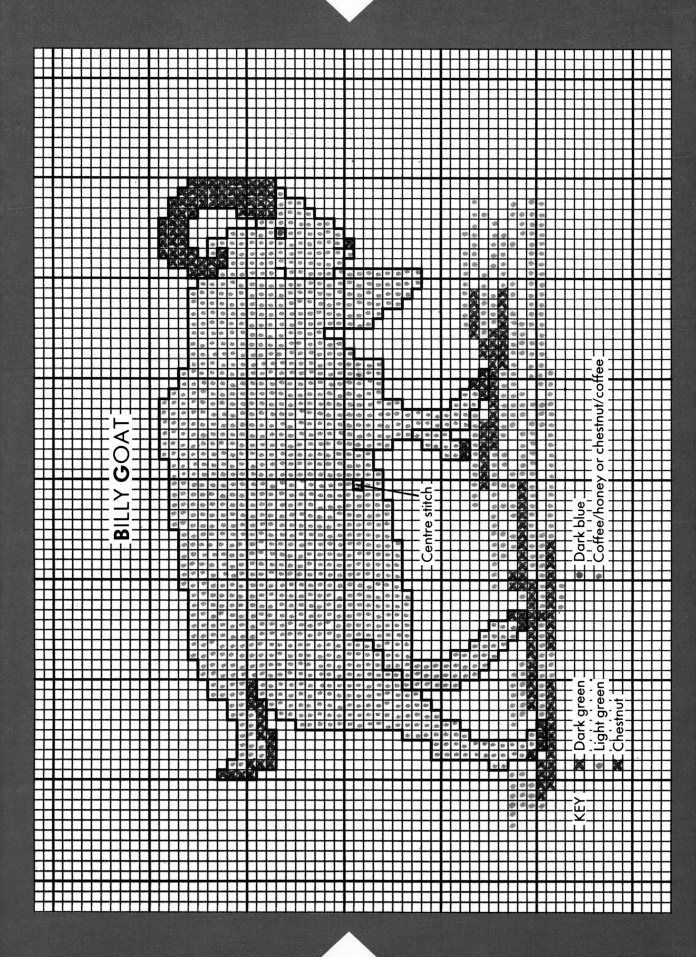

BILLY GOAT

Centre stitch

KEY

● Dark green
● Light green
✕ Chestnut

● Dark blue
● Coffee/honey or chestnut/coffee

GREEN LAND ROVER

THREADS

COLOUR	DMC	ANCHOR
Dark green	561	0216
Dark grey	413	0400
Pale grey	3072	0274
Yellow	725	0306
Light green	562	0210
Dark brown	898	0381

● This farm vehicle is worked in two shades of green, but you could personalise the bodywork to copy other four-wheel drive cars if you like!

STITCHING INSTRUCTIONS

● Cut a piece of Aida fabric not less than 25 x 25cm [10 x 10 inches] and hem the raw edges to prevent fraying [see page 4].
● Mark the centre of the fabric with lines of tacking stitches [see page 5].

● Thread your needle with three strands of light green stranded cotton (floss), look at the chart and, starting from the marked central stitch, work across and up towards the land rover's windscreen, keeping the top stitch of each cross stitch facing in the same direction.
● Using the dark green, add the wheel mudguards and radiator.
● Continue working all the cross stitches in the same way, finishing off the ends as you go [see page 5].
● When the cross stitch is complete, remove the tacking threads marking the centre, check for missed stitches and then add the outlining.

OUTLINING

● Thread your needle with two strands of dark grey stranded cotton (floss) and add the outline in back stitch around the land rover.
● Using two strands of dark grey add the solid lines for the rear view mirror and windscreen guard.

GREEN LAND ROVER

KEY

Dark green
Dark grey
Pale grey
Yellow
Light green
Dark brown

Centre stitch

SMILEY SHEEP

THREADS

COLOUR	DMC	ANCHOR
Black	310	0403
Dark grey	317	0400
Blue	340	0118
Green	367	0216
Brown	407	0914
Honey	738	0372
Coffee	437	0373

● This smiley sheep is stitched quite simply by mixing shades in the needle as with the billy goat [see page 18].

STITCHING INSTRUCTIONS

● Cut a piece of Aida fabric not less than 25 x 20cm [10 x 8 inches] and hem the raw edges to prevent fraying [see page 4].

● Mark the centre of the fabric with lines of tacking stitches [see page 5].

● Thread your needle with two strands of honey and one of coffee stranded cotton (floss) together, look at the chart and, starting from the marked central stitch, work towards the sheep's legs, keeping the top stitch of each cross stitch facing in the same direction.

● When you have finished this needleful, try another combination of colours. You will see that smiley sheep's coat looks more natural than if worked in just one colour.

● Continue working all the cross stitches in the same way, finishing off the ends as you go.

● When the cross stitch is complete, remove the tacking threads marking the centre, check for missed stitches and then add the outlining.

OUTLINING

● Thread your needle with two strands of dark grey stranded cotton (floss) and add the outline in back stitch around the sheep's body.

● Using one strand of black, add the smile and the outline to the face in back stitch.

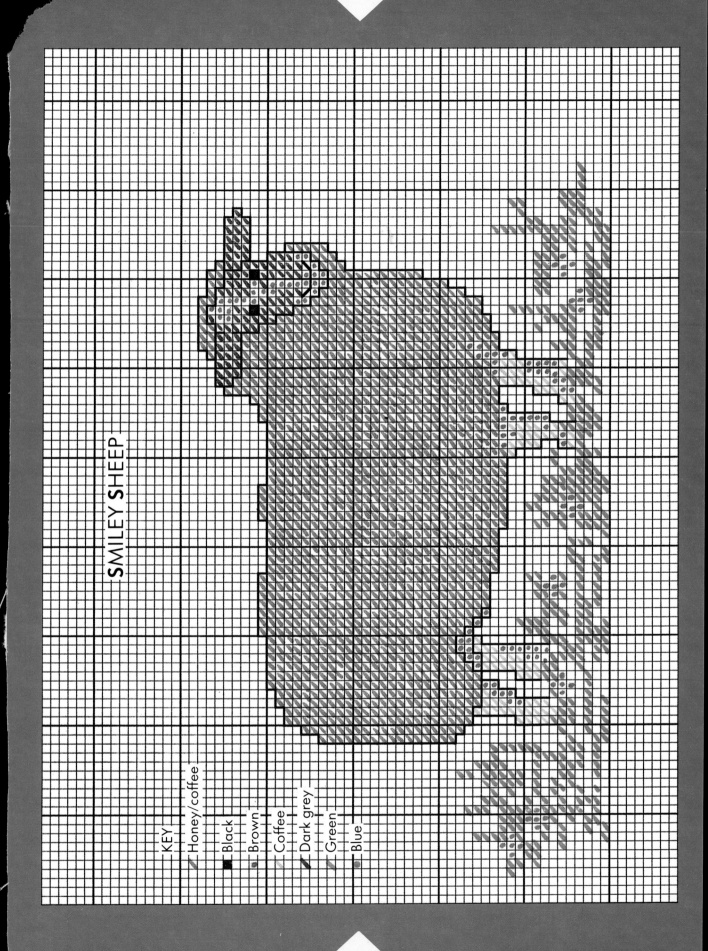

SMILEY SHEEP

KEY

Honey/coffee

■ Black

Brown

Coffee

Dark grey

Green

Blue

design for yourself

Projects Eight, Nine and Ten are intended to give you the opportunity to design for yourself. The beauty of cross stitch is that you can alter designs to suit bigger projects by combining the patterns. You can see this with the charts overleaf, and it is simple to do.

HOW TO DESIGN

In the colour picture opposite there are a number of chickens and little yellow chicks in front of the chicken house. As you can see from the chart, only one of each is illustrated, with the house in the background.

Using a soft pencil and squared paper, copy the outline of the chicken's house and then add the outline of as many chicks and chickens as you want to the drawing.

Cut out the drawn shapes and move them around until you have a pleasing arrangement, then glue them to another sheet of squared paper and follow this new chart to stitch your own masterpiece!

The big farm picture at the front and back of the book was produced in the same way. The tractor from page 13 is combined with the pig family overleaf and the fence and greenery charted on page 29.

It is not necessary to copy all the details from the charts because you can stitch your designs from the book when you have finished planning. The outline should be sufficient.

MEASUREMENTS AND COLOURS

If you choose to make the chicken house and pig family exactly as shown, the sizes of fabric are given. If you make up your own designs, you will need to calculate the amount of fabric needed. For every 11 squares on the chart you will need 2.5cm [1 inch] of 11 count Aida fabric. Remember to add 10cm [4 inches] to both dimensions for the margins.

The colours and shade numbers included in these projects are for your guidance. Why not try experimenting with different colours?

HAPPY DESIGNING!

PROJECT EIGHT

CHICKEN HOUSE

COLOUR	DMC	ANCHOR
Coral pink	351	010
Yellow	725	0306
Dark coffee	434	0365
Dark grey	317	0400
Dark stone	632	0936
Blue	995	0410
Honey	437	0362
Stone	612	0832
Green	562	0210
Coffee	435	0901

STITCHING INSTRUCTIONS

● To make the chicken house as shown, cut a piece of Aida fabric 37 x 27cm [15 x 11 inches] and hem the raw edges to prevent fraying [see page 4]. Otherwise, plan your own version of this design, using the photograph and chart as a guide and referring to Design for Yourself [opposite].

● Mark the centre of the fabric with lines of tacking stitches [see page 5], look at the chart [page 26], thread your needle with three strands of stranded cotton (floss) in the appropriate colour and, starting from the marked central stitch, work the cross stitches in the usual way.

Remember to keep the top stitch of each cross stitch facing in the same direction, and finish off the ends as you go [see page 5].

When the cross stitch is complete, remove the tacking threads marking the centre, check for missed stitches and then add the outlining.

OUTLINING

Thread your needle with two strands of stranded cotton (floss) in the appropriate colour and add the outlines in back stitch.

In the picture above, the chicken house, the mother hen and the chickens are all outlined in dark grey, with the small yellow chicks outlined in coffee.

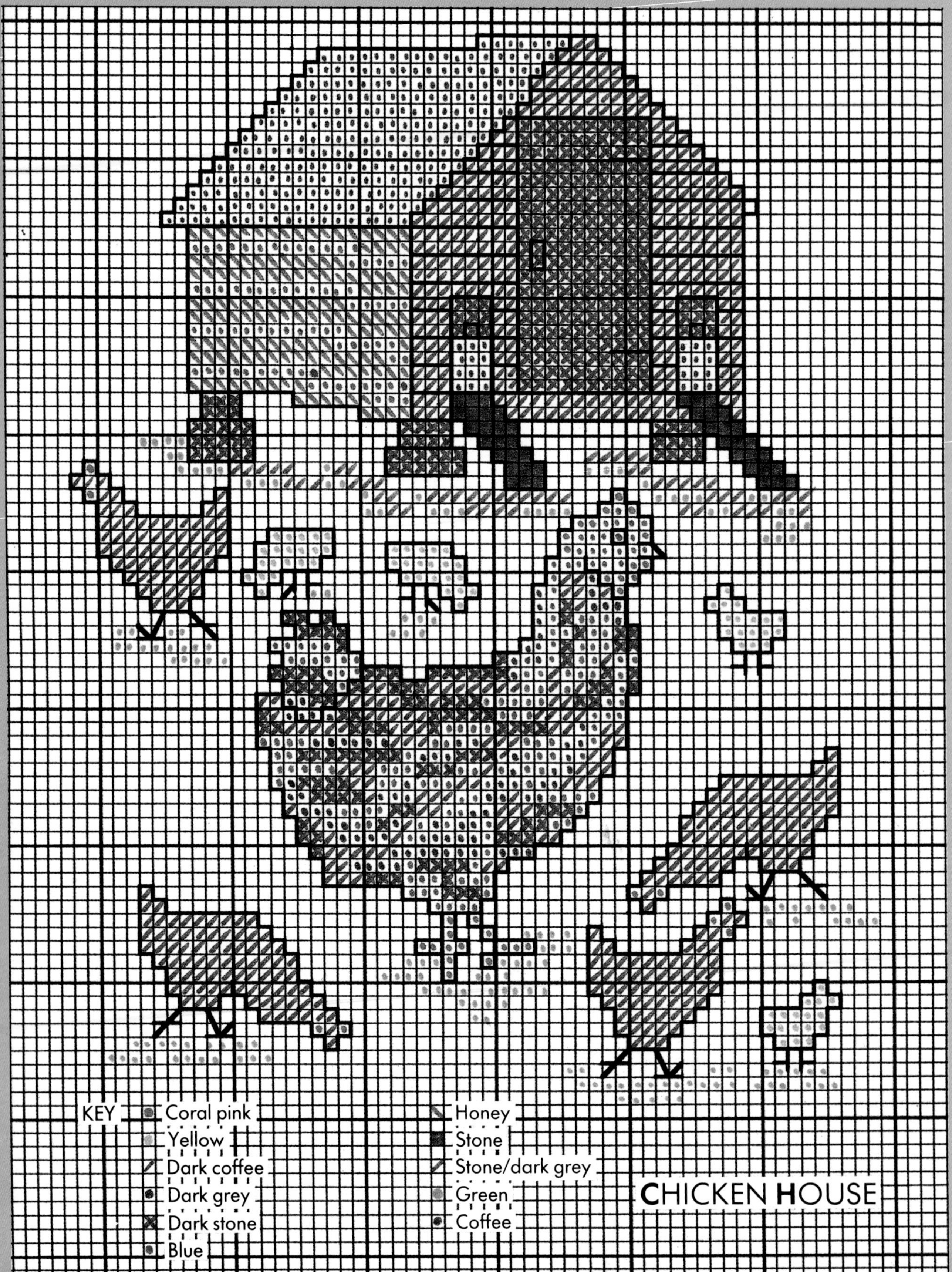

KEY
- Coral pink
- Yellow
- Dark coffee
- Dark grey
- Dark stone
- Blue
- Honey
- Stone
- Stone/dark grey
- Green
- Coffee

CHICKEN HOUSE

how to reverse
a simple design

The picture above illustrates how simple projects can be adapted. The twin billy goats are drawn using a simple reversing method.

Copy the outline of the billy goat from page 19 on to a piece of squared paper. Stick this to a window with a little sticky tape, drawing side to the glass, and you will be able to trace the reversed outline of the goat on another sheet of squared paper!

Then just alter the colours of the second goat and you can produce another project!

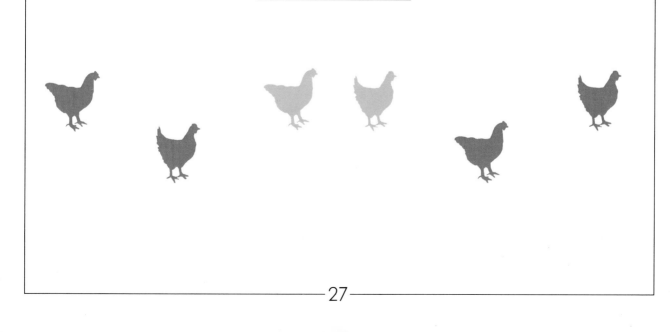

PIG HOUSE AND FAMILY

THREADS

COLOUR	DMC	ANCHOR
Green	367	0216
Sand	834	0874
Pink	352	09
Pale peach	353	06
Dark grey	317	0400
Brown	407	0914
Light green	368	0214
Stone	3032	0392

STITCHING INSTRUCTIONS

● To make the pig family as shown on page 17, cut a piece of Aida fabric 33 x 19cm [13 x 8 inches] and hem the raw edges to prevent fraying [see page 4]. Otherwise, plan your own version of this design, using the photograph and the chart opposite as a guide, and referring to Design for Yourself [page 24]. Why not add more piglets and alter the colours?

● This design uses the pink pig from page 7 and adds three little piglets and an iron pig house to the background. If you would like to add more piglets, remember to increase the size of your piece of fabric.

● Mark the centre of the fabric with lines of tacking stitches [see page 5], look at the chart, thread your needle with three strands of stranded cotton (floss) in the appropriate colour and, starting from the marked central stitch, work the cross stitches in the usual way.

● Remember to keep the top stitch of each cross stitch facing in the same direction, and finish off the ends as you go [see page 5].

● When the cross stitch is complete, remove the tacking threads marking the centre, check for missed stitches and then add the outlining.

OUTLINING

● Thread your needle with two strands of stranded cotton (floss) in the appropriate colour and add the outlines in back stitch.

● In the design pictured opposite, the pig house, the mother pig and her babies are all outlined in dark grey.

THE FARMYARD

● The large project at the front and back of the book shows a farmyard scene. The design is made up using the tractor [page 13], the pig house and family [opposite], the chicken house [page 26] and the farmyard fence and greenery [opposite].

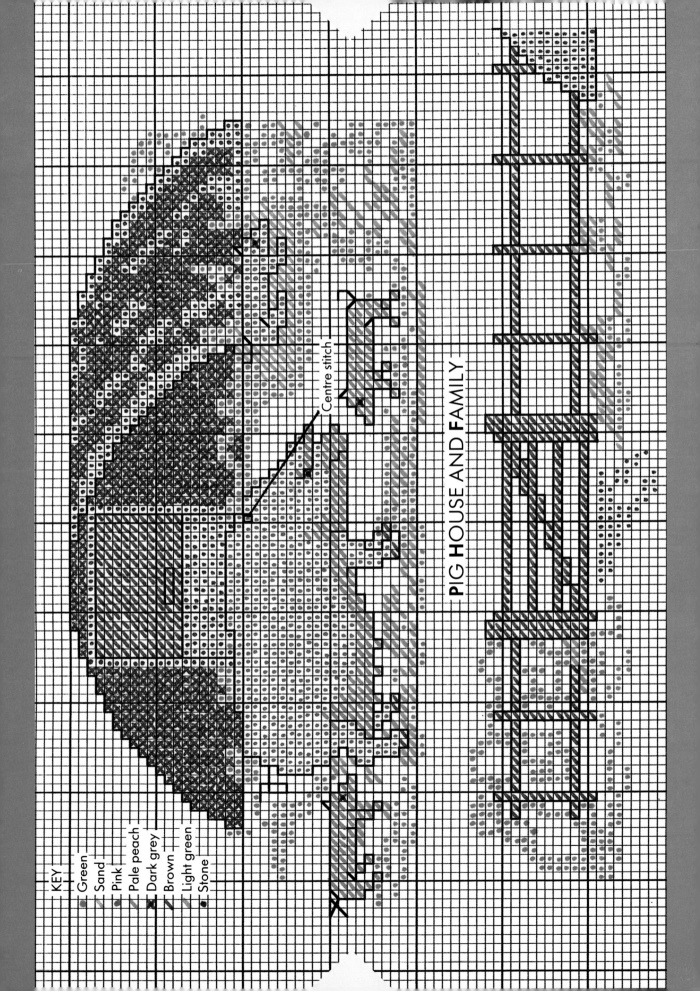

KEY
● Green
⁄ Sand
● Pink
⁄ Pale peach
✗ Dark grey
⁄ Brown
⁄ Light green
● Stone

Centre stitch

PIG HOUSE AND FAMILY

simple mounting and framing

When you have completed a cross stitch design you may wish to make the finished piece into a picture, perhaps to give as a gift.

In some cases a simple 'flexi' frame may be used. These are simple plastic frames made in two parts and the stitching is sandwiched between them. Needlework shops stock many different sizes and colours, so you can choose the best for your design.

If you would like to make your design into a card for a friend, there are dozens to choose from, so you can select the colour and shape of card to suit your stitching. (Follow the manufacturer's instructions.)

If you prefer to make your project into a picture with a rigid frame, you will need to stretch the material to remove any wrinkles and ensure that the stitching is straight! Before you start, wash the stitching if necessary and then iron it [see opposite].

It is not difficult to mount a piece of stitching yourself if you follow the instructions below.

MOUNTING INSTRUCTIONS

You will need:
- stiff card or foam core (available from picture framers)
- glass-headed pins
- double-sided sticky tape
- masking tape
- purchased frame
- scissors
- tape measure or ruler
- pencil

1 Work on a clean, flat surface.
2 Cut a piece of card or board that will fit your frame.
3 Measure the card along the bottom edge and mark the middle with a small pencil mark.
4 Repeat for all four sides.
5 Mark the middle of the bottom edge of the design with a pin and match the two centres.
6 Working from the middle, pin the fabric to the card as shown [see below].
7 Turn the work and pin the opposite side in the same way.
8 Turn to one side and pin from the centre as before.
9 You will then have pins all the way around the card [see below].
10 Check that the design is straight and that you have removed any wrinkles.
11 Turn the work over to the wrong side and, using double-sided sticky tape, stick down the excess fabric, one side at a time [see below].
12 Do not remove all the pins until all the sides are fixed in place.
13 Tape down the raw edges using masking tape and put the mounted stitching into the frame, then fix in position.

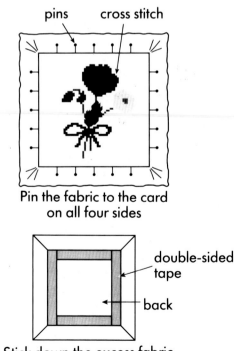

Pin the fabric to the card on all four sides

Stick down the excess fabric

washing and ironing
cross stitch

Here are a few simple tips to follow when you have finished a piece of cross stitch and wonder what to do next.

WASHING

Try to avoid washing your piece at all. Keep your stitching in a safe clean place, away from pets and worst of all, food and drink.

Even in the best-run homes accidents will happen, so it may be necessary to wash a piece of stitching. If you have used either of the brands of thread mentioned in the book, there is no danger of the colour running as long as you wash the item in warm water by hand. Allow the fabric to dry naturally and then press as below [do NOT use the tumble dryer].

IRONING

Before using a hot iron, check with an adult. Ask for help rather than burning your work or, worse still, yourself!

Heat the iron to a hot setting and use the steam button if your iron has one. Cover the ironing board with a THICK layer of towelling. I use four layers of bath towel.

Place the stitching on the towel, right side down, with the back of the work facing you. Press down on the piece firmly.

acknowledgements

I would like to thank all the people who made this book possible. My husband Bill, who continues to support me, often under impossible circumstances! My children James and Louise, who gave me the idea, and Vivienne Wells at David & Charles who still believes in me!
Michel Standley and all the Inglestone Team who keep things running smoothly in my absence. Simon Apps for the super photography.
A special thank-you to the Head Teacher, Jon Allnutt, and to Beryl Booker at Fairford School, Gloucestershire, for all their help and for finding yet another team of excellent stitchers and advisers, without whom this book would not have been possible.
My school advisers were Steven Watson, Christopher Nash, Andrew Knight, Edward Bridges, Kate White, Harriet Hurdle, Rhys Hubbard-Miles, Rachael Goozee, Helen Taylor, Sarah Nicholls, Rebecca Sawyer, Joanna Shaw and Kiera Jones.
Thanks also to my faithful team of stitchers who stitch and check patterns, including Vera Greenoff, Hanne Castelo, Sarah Haines, Su Maddocks, Carol Lebez, Sophie Bartlett, Sarah Day, Jill Vaughan, Christine Banfield, Margaret Cornish, Sharon Griffiths, Barbara Webster, Suzanne Hunt and Jenny Kirby.
And finally, to DMC Creative World for the generous supplies of threads and fabrics, Tunley and Son for framing and art supplies, and Sarah Jane Gillespie for the clever decorative drawings.

index

Numbers in *italics* refer to Charts